115th CONGRESS
1st Session

Commission on Security

KLEPTOCRATS OF THE KREMLIN: TIES BETWEEN BUSINESS AND POWER IN RUSSIA

JULY 20, 2017

**Briefing of the
Commission on Security and Cooperation in Europe**

Washington: 2017

Commission on Security and Cooperation in Europe
234 Ford House Office Building
Washington, DC 20515
202-225-1901
csce@mail.house.gov
http://www.csce.gov
@HelsinkiComm

Legislative Branch Commissioners

HOUSE
CHRISTOPHER H. SMITH, New Jersey
 Co-Chairman
ALCEE L. HASTINGS, Florida
ROBERT B. ADERHOLT, Alabama
MICHAEL C. BURGESS, Texas
STEVE COHEN, Tennessee
RICHARD HUDSON, North Carolina
RANDY HULTGREN, Illinois
SHEILA JACKSON LEE, Texas
GWEN MOORE, Wisconsin

SENATE
ROGER WICKER, Mississippi,
 Chairman
BENJAMIN L. CARDIN. Maryland
JOHN BOOZMAN, Arkansas
CORY GARDNER, Colorado
MARCO RUBIO, Florida
JEANNE SHAHEEN, New Hampshire
THOM TILLIS, North Carolina
TOM UDALL, New Mexico
SHELDON WHITEHOUSE, Rhode Island

Executive Branch Commissioners

Department of State
Department of Defense
Department of Commerce

ABOUT THE ORGANIZATION FOR SECURITY AND COOPERATION IN EUROPE

The Helsinki process, formally titled the Conference on Security and Cooperation in Europe, traces its origin to the signing of the Helsinki Final Act in Finland on August 1, 1975, by the leaders of 33 European countries, the United States and Canada. As of January 1, 1995, the Helsinki process was renamed the Organization for Security and Cooperation in Europe [OSCE]. The membership of the OSCE has expanded to 56 participating States, reflecting the breakup of the Soviet Union, Czechoslovakia, and Yugoslavia.

The OSCE Secretariat is in Vienna, Austria, where weekly meetings of the participating States' permanent representatives are held. In addition, specialized seminars and meetings are convened in various locations. Periodic consultations are held among Senior Officials, Ministers and Heads of State or Government.

Although the OSCE continues to engage in standard setting in the fields of military security, economic and environmental cooperation, and human rights and humanitarian concerns, the Organization is primarily focused on initiatives designed to prevent, manage and resolve conflict within and among the participating States. The Organization deploys numerous missions and field activities located in Southeastern and Eastern Europe, the Caucasus, and Central Asia. The website of the OSCE is: <www.osce.org>.

ABOUT THE COMMISSION ON SECURITY AND COOPERATION IN EUROPE

The Commission on Security and Cooperation in Europe, also known as the Helsinki Commission, is a U.S. Government agency created in 1976 to monitor and encourage compliance by the participating States with their OSCE commitments, with a particular emphasis on human rights.

The Commission consists of nine members from the United States Senate, nine members from the House of Representatives, and one member each from the Departments of State, Defense and Commerce. The positions of Chair and Co-Chair rotate between the Senate and House every two years, when a new Congress convenes. A professional staff assists the Commissioners in their work.

In fulfilling its mandate, the Commission gathers and disseminates relevant information to the U.S. Congress and the public by convening hearings, issuing reports that reflect the views of Members of the Commission and/or its staff, and providing details about the activities of the Helsinki process and developments in OSCE participating States.

The Commission also contributes to the formulation and execution of U.S. policy regarding the OSCE, including through Member and staff participation on U.S. Delegations to OSCE meetings. Members of the Commission have regular contact with parliamentarians, government officials, representatives of non-governmental organizations, and private individuals from participating States. The website of the Commission is: <www.csce.gov>.

KLEPTOCRATS OF THE KREMLIN: TIES BETWEEN BUSINESS AND POWER IN RUSSIA

JULY 20, 2017

PARTICIPANTS

	Page
Paul Massaro, Policy Advisor, Commission on Security and Cooperation in Europe	1
Brian Whitmore, Senior Russia Analyst, Radio Free Europe	2
Ilya Zaslavskiy, Research Expert, Free Russia Foundation	4
Dr. Anders Aslund, Senior Fellow, Atlantic Council	7
Marius Laurinavičius, Senior Analyst, Vilnius Institute for Policy Analysis	9
Ambassador David Fried, Distinguished Fellow, Atlantic Council	11

KLEPTOCRATS OF THE KREMLIN: TIES BETWEEN BUSINESS AND POWER IN RUSSIA

JULY 20, 2017

Commission on Security and Cooperation in Europe
Washington, DC

The briefing was held at 3:32 p.m. in room G11, Dirksen Senate Office Building, Washington, DC, Paul Massaro, Policy Advisor, Commission on Security and Cooperation in Europe, moderating.

Panelists present: Paul Massaro, Policy Advisor, Commission on Security and Cooperation in Europe; Brian Whitmore, Senior Russia Analyst, Radio Free Europe; Ilya Zaslavskiy, Research Expert, Free Russia Foundation; Dr. Anders Aslund, Senior Fellow, Atlantic Council; Marius Laurinavičius, Senior Analyst, Vilnius Institute for Policy Analysis; and Ambassador David Fried, Distinguished Fellow, Atlantic Council.

Mr. MASSARO. All right, then, let's get started.

Full house today. Good afternoon, ladies and gentlemen. Thank you all for coming today. Welcome to today's briefing on kleptocracy in Russia.

My name is Paul Massaro, and I am the policy advisor responsible for economic and environmental issues at the Helsinki Commission.

Combatting corruption is a core imperative of the Organization for Security and Cooperation in Europe, or the OSCE. Corruption takes many forms, but the one that concerns us today is kleptocracy, or rule by thieves. Nowhere is this idea of corruption as a system of government more fully realized than in the Russian Federation.

Russia has been on a steady path to kleptocratic authoritarianism ever since Putin entered the scene 18 years ago. Since then a new generation has entered adulthood, one that does not remember a Russia before Putin. As these young Russian men and women enter the workforce, they confront institutions in both the public and private sectors that have been completely assimilated into Putin's kleptocratic architecture, and are left with a choice to either be co-opted into this corrupt system or ejected from it.

While Putin is the central figure responsible for Russia's descent into kleptocratic rule, he is not the only one. The strongman of the Kremlin is surrounded by a loyal group of cronies who aid and abet the president, complicit in the robbery of the Russian people and the sad state of Russian democracy. Moreover, these cronies enable the Kremlin to export its brand of kleptocracy into neighboring countries, transforming corruption into a potent geostrategic weapon.

Our briefing today will examine the dynamics of Putin's closest circle in order to establish who most strengthens and benefits from his rule. Additionally, briefers will analyze how these cronies advance Putin's goals and interests. We are grateful to have such distinguished panelists with us here today. I look forward to hearing your thoughts on this important issue.

First, we have Brian Whitmore, who joins us all the way from Prague. Brian is a senior Russia analyst for Radio Free Europe/Radio Liberty [RFE/RL], and also writes The Power Vertical blog. Prior to joining RFE/RL in 2007, he worked for eight years for The Boston Globe, first in the Globe's Moscow Bureau and later as a Central and Eastern Europe correspondent based in Prague.

Following Brian, we have Ilya Zaslavskiy—and, Ilya, I understand your wife just had a baby, so thank you so very much for being with us here today—[applause]—rather than at home; you know, we understand what a sacrifice you're making to talk about this very important topic—who joins us from the Free Russia Foundation, where he is a research expert—[laughs]—and Chatham House, where he is an academy associate. In addition, he heads Free Speech LLC, which runs a project on the export of corrosive practices from post-Soviet states to the West.

We'll then hear from Dr. Anders Aslund, who the Helsinki Commission knows very, very well, who is a senior fellow at the Atlantic Council and a professor at Georgetown University. Anders is a leading specialist on economic policy in Russia, Ukraine, and Eastern Europe, and worked as an economic adviser to the president of the Ukraine from 1994 to 1997.

Following Anders, we have Marius Laurinavičius. [Laughter.] Help me out here. These Lithuanian names, man. [Laughter.]

Mr. LAURINAVIČIUS. Laurinavičius.

Mr. MASSARO. OK, that—[Laughter]—who joins us from Vilnius, even further away than Prague. Marius is a senior analyst with the Vilnius Institute for Policy Analysis and a former fellow at the Hudson Institute. A highly regarded journalist from Lithuania, Marius has been reporting on Russian domestic and foreign policy for over two decades.

And finally, we will hear from Ambassador Daniel Fried, distinguished fellow at the Atlantic Council. Ambassador Fried is one of the U.S. Government's foremost experts on Russia and the former Soviet sphere. His career with the Foreign Service has spanned over four decades in seven presidencies—wow—ending earlier this year when he retired from his post as the State Department's coordinator on sanctions policy. So, very relevant for this discussion.

We will conclude with a Q&A session.

I'd like now to give the floor to our first panelist, Brian Whitmore, who will provide us with an overview of the Russian kleptocratic political system. Brian, the floor is yours.

Mr. WHITMORE. Thank you. Thank you, Paul. Thank you for the invitation. It's a great honor to be here. I can't say how delighted I am that this issue is getting attention.

Mr. MASSARO. Oh, get the mic. There you go.

Mr. WHITMORE. There we go. That's better. Should I start again, or did everybody hear me? [Laughter.]

I can't say how delighted I am that this issue is finally getting attention. We've been talking for the last few years a lot about the information war. I've attended more STRATCOM summits and STRATCOM dialogues and STRATCOM seminars than—well, I'm enjoying all of them, but I think—I've been harping on the issue that we need to broaden the aperture here a little bit, because information is just one of the things that the Kremlin has weaponized. And in my opinion, the most important thing they've weaponized is corruption.

I'll start by saying I think it's a bit misleading to characterize Vladimir Putin's Russia as simply a kleptocracy, because this implies that the regime's primary aim is the enrichment of the elite, and I don't think this is the case. In Russia, corruption has been instrumentalized at home and it's been weaponized abroad.

The domestic role of corruption is to control the elite and to maintain its loyalty. Members of the Russian political elite effectively have the license to seek rents, to monetize their positions, so long as they remain politically loyal and politically useful to the Putin regime. Only those who prove disloyal or unuseful are ever prosecuted for corruption.

When there's a corruption case in Russia, the first question I always ask myself is not did he or she do what he or she is accused of doing, because of course they did. I say: Whom did they cross or whom did they cross politically? What happened? Why are they out on the outs politically? What happened here? That's always the first question to ask when a corruption case bubbles up in this regime.

Internationally, corruption has been weaponized and used as a tool of statecraft. The Kremlin seeks to capture elites and establish networks of influence abroad by ensnaring officials in corrupt deals. I'm not going to get into the details here because we want to keep it really brief in the beginning, so I'm going to paint broad strokes and we'll go into details later.

Moreover, the Russian state has both kleptocratic and ideological elements to it. This is what I call the two Russias. Sometimes kleptocratic Russia and ideological Russia do indeed work hand in glove. And by ideological Russia, I mean this project of Putin's to essentially make Russia great again, to bring Russia back up off of its knees and to restore it to what it believes to be its rightful place as a world power. Sometimes corruption and ideology go hand in hand, but at other times the two Russias are in tension with each other and operate at cross purposes.

Closely related to the weaponization of corruption is the weaponization of Russian organized crime, which is also used as a tool of statecraft. But just as it is incorrect to classify Russia as simply an autocracy, it's also incorrect to classify it as a mafia state, as many Kremlin watchers do. More accurately, as my friend and colleague Mark Galeotti wrote in a recent report for the European Council on Foreign Relations, Russia is effectively a state with a nationalized mafia. The Russian security services cooperate closely with organized crime, often facilitating their activities. As a result, the security services are able to establish a so-called *chernaya kassa*, or black account, which has untraceable cash that can be used for all sorts of off-the-book operations, influence operations abroad. And I can go into a little bit more detail about this, but I'll keep my opening remarks brief.

Organized crime groups are often pressed into service to perform tasks the Kremlin wants to keep its fingerprints off, such as smuggling weapons into the Donbas, assassinating troublesome dissidents in London, and so on and so forth.

Weaponized corruption and organized crime are also part of a larger, non-kinetic arsenal that Putin's Kremlin is using to weaken Western institutions. Other elements of this include finance, information, energy, cyberspace, support for extremist political parties, and religion.

If you want to think about the sources of Putin's conduct in this—why is this regime behaving this way—and you look at Putin the man, I like to look at Putin as kind of a hybrid product. "Hybrid" is another one of the words of the past few years. I'm going to put it into a whole new context.

Putin's a hybrid man. It's very stereotypical to look at Putin as a product of the KGB. And I think this is correct, but it's only part of the picture. If genealogically Putin is a product of the Lubyanka, of the KGB, sociologically he is a product of the wild 1990s, of the Darwinian criminal world that existed in cities like St. Petersburg, where he was deputy mayor and played an integral role as a liaison between the city authorities and the city's main organized crime groups in the 1990s. And I think this is something that's very important to understand.

In conclusion, I'll say that one of my favorite talking points is the headline of a piece I passed out to the other panelists here, and that is that "Corruption is the New Communism." The Kremlin's black cash is the new red menace, and it has to be looked at that way. Corruption as a tool of statecraft is something that is spreading from Moscow and is spreading as a tool of influence.

I mean, if you think about this, communism, despite its faults—and, of course, they were legion—did attempt to appeal to universal human ideals and aspirations, although in practice it often worked against these ideals. Corruption, on the other hand, appeals to the most universal and basest human instincts, that of greed. And sadly, it's often in sync with human nature, which makes the new red menace potentially more dangerous and insidious than the old one.

Finally, I'll say corruption today is not just a matter of good governance anymore. It's not something we want to fight just because we want to be honest and good, although we do. Corruption is a national security issue of the highest order and needs to be treated as such.

Thank you.

Mr. MASSARO. Well, thank you very much, Brian, for that fascinating overview, as well as these sorts of elaborations on how the regime exactly is structured—that it's not simply ruled by thieves, it has these ideological components to it. You know, I read your article "Corruption is the New Communism" today, and just an incredible piece. I think that framing the issue in those terms is precisely the way that U.S. foreign policy needs to be approaching this topic.

So, with that, I'll hand the floor to Ilya. Ilya?

Mr. ZASLAVSKIY. Thank you, Paul, and thank you for coming.

As Brian correctly said, finally this topic is out in the open, everyone is discussing it, and actually we quickly transferred from not discussing it to a term which I recently heard, "outrage fatigue," with kleptocracy. Everyone understands the problem, but no one knows how to handle this unbelievable flow of information about kleptocracy and what to actually do with it.

I've been studying this topic since at least 2011, being sort of a junior expert with other people and senior experts from Russia and Europe, warning about national security implications of corruption for the West coming from post-Soviet space. And even before aggression against Ukraine happened, I predicted in 2013 that especially Russian kleptocracy are taking their corrosive practices and corruption to Europe and U.S.—over at least 25 corrupt or corrosive channels, including lobbying, media acquisition, manipulation of information [provided to nations ?], influencing discourse at think tanks and universities, and so forth.

In this briefing, I want to put forward a further warning and prediction. I think the West, especially the U.S. as leader of the democratic world, has been so negligent and appeasing of both Soviet corruption and subversion of democratic values and institutions under Putin over the last 18 years that even on the best-case scenario Russian kleptocracy will not be eradicated in the foreseeable future. The best the West can hope right now, from now on, is to try to attempt to contain negative global impact of rampant kleptocracy coming especially from post-Soviet space, and try preserving its own democratic institutions and values. So, in a nutshell, this problem is really no longer just about Russia or post-Soviet, it's really about the U.S and the West.

In my research paper that is slated to come out at the Kleptocracy Initiative of Hudson Institute in the next month, called—we call it "Neo-Gulag Values and Their Influence in the West," sort of the working title—I really want to emphasize the influence of non-state actors, or supposed non-state actors coming from post-Soviet space. The biggest difference with the Soviet Union is that not only is there this seeming sort of business interactions between supposedly private sector in post-Soviet space and in the West, but the nature of transactions has changed considerably. And there is little understanding, in my view, in the West, despite ample evidence that really from Soviet times we now see a fusion of three different worlds and values coming from post-Soviet space in one elite.

So, in Soviet times, we used to have three different worlds: Communist Party, KGB and different security services and law enforcement, and actual organized crime. They were actually quite antagonistic and conflicting with each other, especially at some important points. But now I would argue that current political elite, especially in Russia but also in surrounding post-Soviet states like Kazakhstan and Azerbaijan, they took the worst but most practical values and business practices from each of the three worlds and amalgamated them into one sort of comprehensive ideology and tactic.

And my friend Karen Dawisha, with her book "Putin's Kleptocracy," my friend investigative journalist Anastasia Kirilenko, they've been showing that especially in St. Petersburg in 1990s, Putin has already tested all these three worlds and practices from those three worlds, and he came to power with a team which has been experienced and used networks from all those three worlds.

I think one of the important conclusions of that study and other studies that we do in Free Russia Foundation is that there are no systemic or any kind of liberals in Russian Government. It's a big myth, which is still somehow spread in Europe, especially in countries like Finland or Germany that still cooperate with Russia on many business levels. So people like Herman Gref, Anatoly Chubais, or Alexei Kudrin have been implicated in those years under Putin even in St. Petersburg, or together with Putin.

I would argue—I mean, recently I highly recommend the study that just came at London's RUSI, and it's emblematic that military and security think tanks raise this question—that shows that Russian-style corporate raiding is one of the most widespread mechanisms of operation of especially big businesses in Russia. Starting from the case of corporate raiding of Yukos, this became a common feature of today's Russia, and Kremlin doesn't want to implement any consistent measures to protect businesses.

Previously, last year, in the report for Free Russia Foundation and Martens Centre in Brussels called "The Tsar and His Business Serfs," I also argue that the term "oligarch" is no longer meaningful, really. In fact, it is a commonly widespread but hugely dangerous mistake in the West to believe that some sort of private businessmen and market economy exist in Russia. They don't. The legal system itself has been hijacked by institutionalized criminal groups, as you said, and security services. And business in Russia really means state favors, tax breaks, contracts from Kremlin, and these "oligarchs" are really now cash handlers of cash flows that are allowed by Putin. And also, Kremlin has special compromising material or other leverage over their lives. Even if these previously conceited oligarchs, they live in the West and appear to be Western businessmen and have looks and lifestyle and lobbyists and lawyer like Western businessmen, they are actually Putin's handlers because their base is in Russia, really. But they want to spend money and sort of enjoy best of two worlds.

This brings me to my second major point in presentation. Kleptocracy in Russia is no longer a case of some distant phenomenon with a residual impact on the U.S. Without any exaggeration, I believe there are strong indicators that we are passing through the times when, as in 1930s, the very existence of liberal Western capitalism with ideals of accountability and good governance are in jeopardy due to the rise of crony or kleptocratic capitalism in post-Soviet space, China, and other developing world. I call this phenomenon G-13 versus G-7 in G-20. In fact, G-7 itself could be not seen as that much about Western liberalism. I mean, if you look at countries like Italy, et cetera.

We see that most developing countries seem to be learning worst kleptocratic government and business practices, and capitalism based on the rule of law and proper separation of powers is no longer an ideal for more societies where people have adapted to sophisticated and often seemingly comfortable and acceptable forms of state-level corruption. So corruption is a new accepted norm on many, many levels in societies, both in the West and in post-Soviet space and elsewhere.

Together with Free Russia Foundation and a group of 2,000 activists around the world, we are preparing the launch of a research project called "Underminers," which you mentioned in my introduction. And I think this is a new term that we believe is more relevant than oligarchs and other non-state actors. It basically shows that we have a whole group of people and actors—non-state actors, but connected with kleptocratic regimes, who actively undermine democracy in the West while enjoying illicit profits in Russia and spending them in the West. I believe these individuals and corporations learnt even more sophisticated financial disinformation and high-tech methods to advance their own interests, and there are multiple examples which I want to go into Q&A session.

What can we do—and if I can have one minute to discuss this—with this outrage fatigue? I think we need a new system of containment against Russian and other post-Soviet kleptocracy that will enforce strictly existing laws, will create more up-to-date laws that deal with today's complex transnational corruption and subversion, especially in regard to anonymous companies and offshore jurisdictions, something which Kleptocracy

Initiative of the Hudson Institute is doing well and many other anti-corruption groups are now discussing in Washington especially. I also think we need to build awareness among Western general public that will create this understanding/acknowledgement in the minds of people about the link between transnational kleptocracy and the erosion of democracy in the West.

So far, I've seen very few actual examples of that. People in London now finally realize that they can't actually live in their own city, especially students and old people, because all these kleptocrats from around the world are raising real estate prices. But we need more examples like this.

And I will finish my presentation with a warning that the price we pay today in the West to stop kleptocracy is considerable, and we have to understand that there will be a price. We need to—especially in the business sector—we need to do containment. We need to really prevent some of the cash flows, especially, but also many, many other different levels of subversion and corruption. But this price is still much smaller than the one that we are likely to be forced to pay tomorrow or the day after tomorrow.

Mr. MASSARO. Well, thank you very much, Ilya. I think your comment that "oligarch" is no longer meaningful is an extremely important point to hit home, especially given that Stephen Colbert recently went to Russia and did his little piece on a day with an oligarch. Well, these oligarchs, they aren't really oligarchs anymore. They're cronies of Putin, that's what they are. You know, it's certainly not like it was, and to a point still is in Ukraine, where the oligarchs have a competitive political environment. These guys aren't competing with one another, they're just working for Putin.

I'd also like to back up your comments on the work of the Kleptocracy Initiative. Give a shout out to Charles Davidson—I see you hiding there in the audience—who's joining us today. He was a panelist at a briefing we did last month, two months ago on asset recovery, and he talked a lot about the corruption services industry in the West, where lawyers and bankers are ready and willing and advertise to take these funds and hide them in the West. So as far as you say so negligent and appeasing, yes, very much so in the West.

With that, I'll hand it over to Dr. Aslund.

Dr. ASLUND. Thank you very much, Paul and the Helsinki Commission, for this invitation.

And indeed, I think that Russia's kleptocracy is a very important topic. When I worked as an economic adviser to the Russian Government in the early 1990s, then my perception of corruption was like this: a pyramid, little at the top and a lot at the bottom. Then, it changed like this. The pyramid was inversed: a lot of corruption at the top, little at the bottom. Russian administration works much better now than it used to—much fewer, small bribes—but now it looks like this. It has become an atomic mushroom, with all the corruption at the top.

And I think that there have been two important things said here: organized crime and oligarchy are over. They have been assumed by the state, and in addition here is to a considerable extent, they have been legalized. President Putin is a lawyer, and he thinks about legalizing many of the things that he's doing. The smaller matter of how the system functions, then whether it's legal or not—I've written several books about Russia's and former—the Soviet Union's economic reforms. Right now, I'm at the final part of a new book with a working title "Russia's Crony Capitalism," and the main idea is very much that Putin has successfully integrated enrichment of the elite in his economic system.

And I will say that I see the Russian economic system today and power system as four different circles. The first circle, that is state power, FSB, and judicial power. There are no independent courts in Russia, therefore, there are no real property rights. Property rights is something that you have abroad, not in Russia. But since you have it abroad, why bother about getting it in Russia? Because it just stops your enrichment.

The second part is the state corporations. Russia's state sector 12 years ago, according to official Russian statistics, generated 35 percent of GDP. Today, it is 70 percent of GDP. The big state companies are buying up the companies from the former oligarchs quickly at half the price because the former oligarchs are no longer allowed to sell to one another or to foreigners. They have to sell to Putin's close friends or to state companies, and then the prices are at most half of what they should be. Therefore, we can see that the prices of Russia's stock exchange are extremely low. If you take the most outstanding state corporate company, Gazprom, it was worth, at the peak, on the London Stock Exchange, $369 billion. Today they have wasted $320 billion. It's down to $50 billion. And this is an extreme example, but it's not untypical.

And in 2007, Putin did something quite extraordinary. He transformed six big state companies with one law from each of them to state corporations which are called nongovernmental organizations, so effectively privatized assets of more than $1 billion of value. And then you wonder who controls these nongovernmental organizations, or *nekommercheskie organizatsii*, as the Russian terms run? Well, of course, it's Putin who controls it all.

And at the third circle, that is the cronies. Four of them have been sanctioned by the U.S. Government: Gennady Timchenko, Arkady and Boris Rotenberg, and Yury Kovalchuk. This is the real Putin circle. These are not KGB people, and they don't work in state companies. They are Putin's real friends, whom the U.S. Government assumes also holds a part of Putin's wealth.

Look, analyzing this, you wonder, how do they make the money? Essentially two ways. Asset stripping, mainly from Gazprom—that is, they buy assets—for example, financial companies and television companies for Gazprom cheaply—and the other is that they get big state procurement orders at massively inflated prices. And there's no competition because these are Putin's friends. Everybody knows what they should be given it.

Looking at the numbers, I come to the assessment that 10 [billion dollars] to $20 billion a year has been taken out by this group of essentially half a dozen people each year since 2006. So if you add it up, we have, only in this way, 100 [billion dollars] to $200 billion that has been taken out by this small group of people. Of course, a consequence of this is there's not much corrupt revenues left for the others. So corruption in Russia today, if we call it like that—because, really, it's quite legalized—they have got these state procurements legally. It's very concentrated.

But what I will shock you with is the fourth circle. Ilya touched up on it, but that is the West. This would not happen in the way it does without the West. After this money goes through Cyprus—but Cyprus is only a channel—and then it goes normally to some Caribbean Island. British Virgin Islands is typical for this. But when it goes to two places—London and New York—or the U.S. more broadly—it goes through anonymous companies, LLCs that are usually in Delaware. They can also be in Nevada, Wyoming, and South Dakota. This should not happen, but it does.

And the other problem is that the money passes not through the bank system—which is properly regulated—but through law firms; fine, well-renowned law firms which consider this to be attorney-client privilege. And in this way, the Wall Street Journal had an article on the 26th of December last year where they assess that at least $40 billion a year goes into this country in this fashion. These are the two things that I suggest that we should focus on stopping. There should be no anonymous companies whose beneficiary owners are not known and there should be absolutely not any accepted transfers of money through law firms that bypasses the bank system. These are the two suggestions I have that the United States Congress should really do something about.

Thank you.

Mr. MASSARO. Well, thank you very much for that comprehensive analysis, Dr. Aslund. You've been such a wealth of knowledge for the Commission for so long. Thanks once again for running us through such an important thing.

Now to reiterate your circles, one is state power, FSB; two is state corporations; three are the cronies and friends of Putin; and then, finally, four is us. A lot to digest.

Marius, the floor is yours.

Mr. LAURINAVIČIUS. Thank you, Paul.

I'd like to thank the organizers for having me here, and I would like to give a credit to two other institutions, first of all to Kleptocracy Initiative I already mentioned. I worked for them for a year and wrote a report for them on weaponizing the kleptocracy, how Putin weaponizes kleptocracy. And I really believe these guys at the Kleptocracy Initiative—not to offend anyone else, but they are the best in terms of expertise and determination to work on the issue.

The other institution I would like to mention is the institution I'm affiliated with right now, Vilnius Institute for Policy Analysis. They sponsored my trip here to D.C., and because of them I am talking and sharing my expertise with you today.

I really think that we in the region, in the Baltic region, in the Eastern Europe, we have something to share with you because almost everything you are experiencing here in United States or in the Western Europe we have experienced already. I mean, everything—information war, kleptocracy, kleptocratic influence, economic influence, you name it. Everything we have experienced already. So I will try to speak today about this particular experience, because I believe you will find some parallels with the processes in the West yourself.

First of all, I would like to say that I was asked to talk about kleptocracy as a tool of foreign policy of Russian regime. I should say it's not a tool of foreign policy, it's a weapon. Putin—it's not only Putin. It's not just about Putin. It's about the system. But Putin's regime weaponizes kleptocracy, and it's not only about foreign policy. It's not only about certain goals of foreign policy.

The second thing is that—and it was already mentioned—we're dealing with not—I should say not a normal state or even not a normal authoritarian state. We're dealing with a mafia state, and that makes a difference. So they're rejecting all kinds of influence which is not usual to normal state influence, and kleptocracy is one of them.

So, talking about our experience, Ilya said that he started to be interested in the topic of kleptocracy in 2013. I should say I started to be interested and work on this in

2003. [Laughter.] And it was because—I don't know how many of you know, but we in Lithuania, we have the worst—the first president—the first impeached president in Europe in the whole history of Europe. So it was 2003 when the scandal broke in Lithuania about the ties of our president to Russian business and even criminals, and that was real eye opening for me, myself. I've been working on Russia since 1991, so it's already 26 years, and it was really eye opening because we found that the influence can be projected by these relations, which at that time were considered just normal business; by the relations to the criminals, because on the list of the people who were related to people around our president were people like Kikalishvili, who was on the U.S. list—well, not sanctions list, but he was on the FBI list.

So I started to work on that. And later I looked back to the history, and I should say that this crony capitalism or kleptocracy in Russia—it started not in the year 2000, when Putin came to power, it started at least in 1991. Or I would say it started even earlier, when Communist Party and KGB made plans to transfer money—huge amounts of money; there are different calculations, but at least 50 billion dollars were transferred to the West, and up to 100 billions of dollars. So, since that, they are projecting the influence over the West using this money, and using this influence and networks of influence.

The other example I would like to give you is from our neighboring country, Latvia. Now we have a coalition in Latvia which is led by the party of the mayor of Ventspils. The name of the guy is Lembergs. And what is interesting about him—he is definitely not called or named pro-Russian or a Russian agent, but what is interesting about him, he started his business in 1991 with the guy who was already mentioned, Timchenko.

And why they are doing this? They try to—not just to achieve some foreign policy goals, they try to capture, as it was said by Brian, elites of the countries. They try to capture institutions. And the ultimate goal is, if it's possible, to capture the entire state.

So, first of all, they captured, of course, not only by having these relations with the mayor of Ventspils, Lembergs, but via the other peoples, they captured the port of Ventspils. And now they have, looking—again, looking back to history, I can say that they projected the Russian influence through several governments of Latvia which were not called pro-Russian. The others, prime ministers of Latvia like Skele or Slesers, they have clear business relations with Russia and always were, well, at least semi-pro-Russian.

But the thing is that, when we don't—we don't call Mr.—let's say Mr. Lembergs as a pro-Russian, we should remember that he was the guy who publicly called Russian troops in Latvia as occupational ones. And the thing is that no one cares about that and no one looks into the history of his business.

The same thing, I should say, about our—well, even U.S. attitude in 2003, because it was a really weird situation when we were talking—in Lithuania, we were talking about Russian influence over Lithuania. And staunchest supporter of Mr. Paksas, the impeached president, at that time was the U.S. ambassador in Vilnius. Every day or every second day he went publicly to defend our president, saying that he's a normal guy, pro-Western, and it's just about politics not about Russian influence. And working on the Kleptocracy Initiative, I put several documents at the kleptocracy archives on the issue, so you can find them yourself.

But, to make it to the end, I should say that we should look at the issue having in mind the quotation of the famous Spanish prosecutor José Grinda. I don't remember the exact quotation, but he said about the network of criminals working for Russian regime—

he said when Russian state can't for one reason or another achieve something by the means of the state, they employ criminals. So, in the same manner, they employ kleptocracy to achieve some goals the state can't achieve itself.

Thank you.

Mr. MASSARO. Absolutely. And thank you, Marius, especially for that in-depth look at the perspective of how far back this all goes. I mean, I think that is the most surprising thing, is starting in 1991 and now, in 2017, we're finally taking an in-depth look at it.

Finally, we have Ambassador Daniel Fried, who's going to talk a little bit about what the United States might be able to do about this.

Amb. FRIED. Thank you.

My point of departure is to assume that the previous speakers are correct about the nature of Russian kleptocracy and its weaponization at the hands of the Putin regime. I make this assumption because I agree with it, but I need not go over the ground that has been covered.

What, then, do we do? First of all, as was the case during the Cold War, nothing will work if we lose the political and, may I say, ideological struggle. We need to have faith in our own democratic system, in ourselves, in the free world. And when we do that, we have a foundation from which to proceed.

I say this because now that very foundation is also under attack, both from without—from the Russians—but principally from within, from people not necessarily at all connected with Russia. So this is a different kind of a struggle. It's not my purpose to go into that, but I want to mention it.

Secondly, a U.S. policy designed to push back against Russian kleptocracy and corruption needs to be integrated in a complete Russia policy. There is nothing incompatible between pushing back on Russian aggression in various forms and seeking those areas of common grounds where it may be possible. I wouldn't be too hopeful about the positive agenda, but you don't rule it out.

Another point is that this is not—as Mr. Laurinavicius pointed out—the Americans may have discovered this recently, but this has been a problem well before we discovered this on the front pages of our newspapers. The Europeans have been dealing with this for a long time, and the Baltic states and Poland have—Bulgaria—have been dealing with it since 1991, essentially. So the answer should not be made in the U.S.; it's got to be coordinated with Europe in particular, and within the G-7, all right?

That said, what are our options? The first is exposure. We should not let the corruption take place in the shadows, in the darkness. And this is a job principally for nongovernmental organizations—for journalists, for the 21st-century cadre of investigative journalists, and that sort of means tech-savvy younger people who are adept at exposing malign influence. They're all over, including in Russia itself. We need to expose what the Russians are doing, the better to anathematize it. Just as it was not popular in the United States to be associated with the Soviet Union as their agent or as their useful idiot, there should be a price to be paid for doing the Kremlin's work for it.

Third—and this is more in the area of government—there is pressure. There are both sanctions and there are enforcement of financial regulations. Treasury's FinCEN, the Financial Crimes Enforcement Network, is not a sanctions organization, but it goes after financial crimes. They're very good. They need to be—their expertise and their resources can be useful in exposing what the Russians are doing.

Fourth—and this requires some discussion—but Russian investment is often, let us say, strategic. They want to buy up key elements of a country's infrastructure using cutouts—Cypriot money, false fronts. In the United States, there is a Committee on Foreign Investment which screens it for national security purposes, so-called CFIUS. It works. It may be that European countries should study that and learn from the example. I understand a body like that can be a hindrance and a bureaucracy to legitimate foreign investment, but when you're dealing with money that isn't what it claims to be, governments may want to provide themselves with protection.

Now, sanctions may have a place here. My last job in government was the State Department's sanctions coordinator. I don't want to overestimate or oversell the ability of sanctions to solve the problem. Still, it is a useful tool.

The Magnitsky Act was not designed to go after corrupt officials. It was designed to go after major human rights abusers. But it turns out we know from the Panama Papers that the corruption that Sergei Magnitsky, the Russian lawyer who was basically murdered because he had uncovered corruption, had uncovered a lot more than we even realized at first. See the Panama Papers, the Prevezon case. When you pull on a Russian thread, you never know what comes out the other end.

The Magnitsky Act seems to bother the Russians, so much so that they want to talk with—about adoptions with just about anybody, adoptions being the euphemism for the deal it would take to roll back the Magnitsky Act, because the Russians imposed a ban on adoptions—American adoptions of Russian children as retaliation. So when you hear someone's talking adoptions with the Russians, what it really means is they're talking about getting rid of Magnitsky. The Magnitsky Act was not designed to deal with this problem, but it stumbled into it because threads in Russia tend to lead to one another.

The Global Magnitsky Act, Senator Cardin's creation in a way, does explicitly deal with corruption. It is a legislative vehicle, now a law, which allows for us to go after corrupt Russian officials. In my experience, it is hard to demonstrate this. But that means you go to work, including with nongovernment sources of information, this army of investigative bloggers and tech-savvy people I mentioned earlier.

The Ukrainian sanctions went after—as Anders said, went after Putin's cronies by design. We were not intending to make things pleasant for the Kremlin after it had invaded one of its neighbors for the second time in 10 years.

The Senate bill, which passed 98–2, which is now being taken up in the House—the Senate bill on Russia sanctions includes among its many provisions two sub-provisions dealing with corruption, one on privatization, allowing the administration to go after individuals who unjustly benefit from privatization—again, maybe hard to demonstrate, but it is a useful vehicle—and more generally corruption, similar to the Global Magnitsky Act. Sanctions are not going to solve the problem, but they are a useful tool.

I mentioned the various threads that come together. All of the tools I mentioned are useful to the degree that we Americans and the Europeans and the G-7 take seriously the challenge of an autocratic Russia which wants to export its corruption and seems to be aiming to make the world safe for Russian autocracy—that is, by weakening democratic institutions and weakening the idea of democracy. And lest you think that's an original thought on my part, it's actually about a 200-year-old Russian policy, from the time of Nicholas the First. No need to remind a Lithuanian about Tsar Nicholas, who used his army to crush every liberal revolution it could reach, the better to keep out the infectious ideas of the Enlightenment.

I do not believe that Russia is doomed to live forever its worst history. I don't accept the notion of a civilizational divide. In Russian history, Russia does, when it fails at external aggression, turn to internal reform, and has sometimes been successful. And the period of Russian history we think of as the most successful, the period that gave us world-class literature and art and music, and a rapidly developing economy, and the beginning of a more modern economic system, came as a result of the failure of its aggression and failure in various wars—Crimean War, Russo-Japanese War. I mention this because it is important to remember what it is we are trying to achieve. We are not trying to achieve a weakening of Russia. We are trying to achieve a defeat of Putinist Russia, the better to have a better relationship with that better Russia. That's my view; Lithuania, being a neighbor of Russia, may have a more jaundiced view of Russian history.

Mr. LAURINAVIČIUS. I couldn't agree more.

Amb. FRIED. OK, good. [Laughter.]

But remember, the current era reminds me more than any other period of the early 1980s, when Russia was hostile to the West, everyone in Europe was worried about the outbreak of war, and Russians were beginning to whisper to Americans in the Soviet Union—I was one of them—things cannot go on like this. The Reagan Administration's approach to Russia had two periods: pressure before Gorbachev; and when the Russians turned inward, having failed to intimidate the West, Reagan abandoned his more rigid cohort and reached out to Gorbachev. And it may be that one of these years a Russian attempt at internal reform will, in fact, succeed.

So rather than end on a note of toughness and hitting back at the Russians, I wanted to talk about at least the potential of a better future. That time will come, though it's not today.

Mr. MASSARO. Well, thank you very much, Ambassador Fried. You know, great talk. Let me add, for the much deeper perspective, going back to the 1980s but also going back 200 years—[laughs]—and also, conversely, for the shout out to the role of young people in getting this done, both tech-savvy and politically engaged, because I know there are a lot of politically engaged young people in this room.

And that leads to my first question. We'll now enter the question-and-answer phase. And this one is for Ilya. In March and June, major protests against corruption broke out, led by Alexei Navalny, leading to crackdowns and imprisonments. Does this signify cracks in the foundation of Putin's kleptocracy, or is this a flash in the pan? And what more can be done to provide assistance to those Russians who want to see a democratic, human rights-respecting Russia in the future?

Mr. ZASLAVSKIY. It's a good question that all Russians ask themselves, and they're divided now, as Russian opposition's often divided on many issues. This is the newest one.

I would say it's definitely a hopeful sign that this new generation of senior students from school and students from universities are really fed up, with no prospects in life and no social mobility and out—rampant corruption that they face and a huge brain drain and immigration out of Russia as the only option to really succeed.

The question is how sustained these protests can be and how much resistance these young people can provide, because one thing that is not realized in the West, I think, enough is that Russia since Soviet times has really traumatic experience of state oppression and Stalinist repressions. And that's why I call—in my report I call this neo-gulag values, because gulag is really a system of prisons and repression, and Russia's—it's a defining feature of Russian culture and political culture as well. And it's nothing cowardly to say that people fear repression, and there is a limit to how much people can withstand. Many of us in this room, including myself, have had to leave Russia because we faced unprecedented dangers to our lives.

I would say the good way to support is, firstly, for the West to uphold its own values but also to engage in what I would call filtered containment. So definitely keep people-to-people contacts and programs. I myself in 1990 participated in a program called FREEDOM Support Act, sponsored by Senator Bradley in the U.S. Congress, and I saw thousands of students from post-Soviet countries coming to the U.S., learning and then becoming long-term advocates of democracy in their own countries, even if they couldn't really enforce their views in political life.

So it's a long-term game. I would say—I agree with Ambassador Fried that one day this regime will collapse, and it's inevitable. But the question is how—it may take a decade or 15 years or lifetime of these kleptocrats that are currently in power. It's a long game, which requires a multilayered approach.

Mr. MASSARO. Thanks very much, Ilya. Dr. Aslund?

Dr. ASLUND. Yes, three comments about Navalny and the protest. The first is that he's focusing on one theme—I think this is very wise—the top theme, corruption. It's not about what kind of reforms that should be done afterwards. I think this is very wise. This is what you do when you want a democratic breakthrough.

The second is that learning from the protests 2011, 2012 that were very concentrated in Moscow and did not excite the rest of Russia—and Navalny is now trying to engage 200 different cities around Russia, the whole country, and as Ilya said, he's focusing on the young.

And the third is quite interesting. He's criticizing one specific person after the other, but not Putin. Boris Nemtsov went after Putin, and we know what happened to him.

Thank you.

Mr. MASSARO. Well, thank you very much. Given that we are coming up to our time constraints here, let's have a whole half hour for audience questions. I'll refrain from asking a second question.

Audience, please. Hands. Over there.

QUESTIONER. All right. Thank you. My question is to the ambassador. You mentioned that Russia in times of failure has turned to internal reform. What would that look like in the Putin administration?

Amb. FRIED. Well, I don't know what it would look like in the Putin administration, but—a Russia reform package would have to involve getting rid of the kleptocracy, opening up the economy, the rule of law at home, and all supported by a better relationship with the West.

The Russian economic reformers, such as they are, make the case that it is precisely Russia's hostile relationship with the West and the failure of the rule of law at home which keep the economy backward and dependent on the export of raw materials.

So you would have a series of liberalizing reforms at home and an anticorruption campaign. That is a little bit hard to imagine under the current leadership, only because

President Putin has a bit of the King Lear problem: You can't go into retirement after you've done the things you've done to stay king. [Laughter.]

But you know, Anders Aslund is the person who knows the state of Russian economic reform thinking and can do a better job answering sort of the content of what a reform package would look like.

Mr. MASSARO. Dr. Aslund?

Dr. ASLUND. Well, I would rather say that first you need to get rid of the regime. You can't change anything where the people are all dependent on a corrupt system. You have to change the people, the leadership. That's the only way.

And in order to do that, you need democratic elections, early democratic elections of both president and the parliament and then lower down after that. The economic reform we know how to do. That's not a big problem.

Mr. MASSARO. Additional questions? Right there. Right next to you, Katya.

QUESTIONER. I wanted to call attention to the best and the worst of Russia. One, to stress the best, today is Lyudmila Alexeyeva's 90th birthday. For those who don't know her name, she's the longstanding chairwoman of the Moscow Helsinki Group and usually referred to as the doyenne of the Russian and, before that, the Soviet human rights movement.

I wanted to ask a question to—perhaps to Anders about something—a rumor I've heard for many years, which is that Putin is probably the richest man in the world. For many years I heard that he's worth 70 billion [dollars]. Now I've heard an updated figure of 120 billion [dollars].

You pointed out why people inside Russia unfortunately don't seem to be able to afford, literally or figuratively, to refer to that fact, if it is a fact, but I wanted to get your reaction to that.

Thank you.

Mr. MASSARO. Before Dr. Aslund speaks, do you mind giving your name and organization? I know who you are, but if——

QUESTIONER. Well, the previous speaker didn't, so I didn't either.

Mr. MASSARO. Right. Yes, sorry, that was my fault. I should have brought that up.

QUESTIONER. Cathy Cosman. I'm recently retired from the U.S. Commission on International Religious Freedom.

Mr. MASSARO. All right. Great.

And if all audience members could do that, that'd be great. Thanks.

Dr. Aslund?

Dr. ASLUND. The simple answer is that we don't know. I think that something in the order of $100 billion would be reasonable.

As I suggested, the Putin group takes out $10 [billion] to $20 billion of Russia each year. What we know from Sergei Kolesnikov, who was a minor partner in one of the branches of a Putin scheme—he was involved in 32 offshore companies, and he fled the country, 2011, afraid of losing his life—what he said was that normally Putin owns about one-third in each company and that he really owns it directly.

So if you take $200 billion and give him one-third, that would—something like $70 billion in that chunk would make sense. But we can't know. We have no idea how many anonymous companies there are in the country.

In Britain Prime Minister David Cameron said a bit more than a year ago that there were 99,000 buildings in Britain that were owned by anonymous companies. And these are normally buildings that cost several million dollars each. So this is a lot of money.

Mr. MASSARO. Marius?

Mr. LAURINAVIČIUS. I have some things to add to that.

To my mind, it's a bit misleading to focus just on Putin, because we are usually doing this mistake in the West that it's about Putin, it's Putin's regime, it's about Putin's wealth, it's about Putin's cronies.

I would say it's much more about the system itself. And the system is based on KGB. It's still based on KGB. It's not just—well, of course it's a hybrid system. It's not just KGB, but it's based on KGB.

And looking to the history, even in years of 1990s, early 1990s, somebody already mentioned that when this, well, symbiosis of KGB and mafia took place, I should say that looking even back to the history, we should say that all these *Vory v Zakone* chiefs—"thieves-in-law"—were controlled by KGB in the Soviet times.

So it's the really based on the KGB, and the KGB managed from the—as I said, we should look at the year of 1991, 1990—what they did at that time. And they managed to come back to power in just 10 years.

Even answering the previous question, to break the regime, we need to do something with all the system, not just Putin or his cronies.

Mr. MASSARO. Thank you.

Additional questions? Right here.

QUESTIONER. Hello. My name is Ellen, and I'm an intern for Senator Gillibrand.

I think my question is directed to Dr. Aslund and Mr. Whitmore. I'm just wondering if you guys could discuss more about how kleptocracies, specifically with business ties and the transfer of money, can lead to the undermining of democracy.

Mr. MASSARO. I guess we'll start with Brian here, and you'll be up next.

Mr. WHITMORE. I can give you an example. Back in 2010 I was researching an article I ultimately coauthored that was published in The New Republic, called "The Velvet Surrender." And it was looking at Russian influence in the Czech Republic in networks of influence. And I came across this company called Vemex. It was an energy trading company with a mindbogglingly opaque ownership structure that ultimately led to Gazprom. This company, Vemex, had bought up 10 to 12 percent of the Czech energy market, and those with ties to it were, unsurprisingly, supportive of the Kremlin line.

Vemex is—oh, let me get—I actually broke this down, because it's pretty complicated. Vemex is owned by companies based in Switzerland, Germany and Austria, one of which is Centrex Europe in Energy and Gas, which is founded by Gazprom's financing arm and registered in Austria and, according to the European Commission, is owned by two companies, one registered in Cyprus and the other controlled by Gazprom's German subsidiary.

Are you confused? Good. That's the point. [Laughs.]

My late colleague Roman Kupchinsky, the former director of RFE/RL's Ukrainian service, testified before the Senate Foreign Relations Committee back in 2008 that Centrex was just one of these companies. Gazprom, with the silent support of the Kremlin, has set up 50 or middlemen companies like this throughout Europe.

Now why is this undermining democracy, to get to your question? Every one of these creates a network of influence that is undermining the rule of law in every one of these countries. I called my article about the Czech Republic "The Velvet Surrender" basically because you had the Velvet Revolution, which brought in democracy. Well, now democracy to an extent was being undermined and surrendered by the presence of these shell companies and the networks of influence that they created.

I've noticed, over time, as these companies have proliferated, other things have also proliferated. You've had many so-called alternative news sites pop up in Central Europe with similarly opaque ownership structures, which, not surprisingly, have a very Euroskeptic line, a very anti-American line, a very pro-Kremlin line. I don't think these things are—I think these things are not unrelated to each other.

So when—I mean, corruption undermines our most basic values, and I wanted to kind of riff off something Ilya said, where you said it's the G-7 versus the G-13. This is a very elegant way of saying something that—a theme that I've been playing with recently. I mean, we're not in a new Cold War right now. We're in a system—but we do have two normative systems essentially facing off against each other in the world. I like the way you put this, the G-7 versus the G-13, because it's a very elegant way to say it. One, to the west, is based on all these things we hold near and dear but appear to be under assault right now: the rule of law, the accountability of government, the sanctity of contracts, the subordination of power to the law. Then we have one to the east based on the things we're talking about on this panel today: cronyism, kleptocracy, the subordination of the law to power.

Now unlike in the Cold War, we don't have two hermetically sealed systems. These things are not separated by a Fulda Gap or an Iron Curtain or a Berlin Wall. They are seeping into each other. And our values are, let's face it, attractive, and they do seep into the other side. The other side is forcing their values into our system, to the extent that we let them, and that's the operative phrase, "to the extent that we let them."

So I hope that addresses your question, but this is how I see corruption undermining democratic values right now and why I see it as a national security threat of the first order.

Mr. MASSARO. Thanks, Brian. Dr. Aslund?

Dr. ASLUND. Yes, let me continue with three examples. The most innocuous is Gerhard Schroeder, the former chancellor of Germany, who is—immediately after he left as the chancellor of Germany became hired by Gazprom through Nord Stream, the gas pipeline. So he's legally paid big money, and he's still an important person in German politics. This is all legal.

Second example: When Putin was prime minister, 2008 to 2012, he spent a large part of his time visiting various countries in all the Balkans, trying to promote South Stream. Whenever I see Putin one-on-one without any aides with a political leader, I immediately suspect that corruption is the real matter there. [Laughter.] Of course, I can't know that.

And the third example is Dmitry Firtash, the odious gas trader in Ukraine. And here you have a really crude case. Reuters published a wonderful article two years ago called "Comrade Criminal." And they described how Dmitry Firtash got a credit line from Gazprom Bank for $11 billion. And for this money, he was allowed to buy gas cheaply in Russia and sell it for billions of dollars of sheer profit in Ukraine at a normal price. And then he was the main or—cofinanced the President Yanukovych election campaign for president in 2010 and 2012. A reasonable guess is that each of these cost him half a billion dollars. Ukrainian elections are very expensive, almost like American elections. [Laughter.] And of course Yanukovych was elected.

So who is Firtash? Essentially this is a Russian agent who's called a gas trader because he carries out political operations to the benefit of Moscow. I might mention also that he was the financier of the Holodomor monument here, just beside the Congress, for $2.5 million a couple of years ago.

Mr. MASSARO. Thank you, Dr. Aslund. Marius, did you want to speak?

Mr. LAURINAVIČIUS. Just to follow up on that, if you follow any story on undermining democracy in Europe or here in the U.S., you will find some Russian money behind that. Absolutely, because if you will take any support for anti-European practice in Europe, you will find that not a state-funded support. You will always find it's an oligarch or a Russian bank or something like that behind that. It's not state-funded.

If you will look to, let's say, the gathering of fascist movements in Moscow, they are doing that every year. So it is financed by Russian oligarchs.

If you will look at the support to—let's take United States—to the secessionist movements in the United States, you will find Russian money and Russian oligarchs behind that. And it's not a funny issue. I really encourage all of you to look at the issue of secessionist movements and Russian support to them, because I really remember when we in Europe, we looked at the issue of Russian support to anti-European parties some seven, eight years ago, and we laughed at that. We thought that it's a funny issue. Now we know that these are, well, movements and Russian support managed to—almost to, well, get to the brink of ruining of European Union.

Mr. MASSARO. Yes, that seems to be the theme. Ambassador Fried.

Amb. FRIED. I agree that you will find Russian money behind many of the anti-European nationalist parties. But let us say France's Front National is not anti-European and nationalist because it receives Russian money. It receives Russian money because that's what it is already, which suggests that the way to solve this and to make our societies less vulnerable to that kind of interference is to work on the issues that brought the West to its current pass, where we are vulnerable to these arguments. It's not to take issue with the question of Russian money, but we—the Russians didn't cause our problem; they're merely feeding on it and contributing to it.

Mr. MASSARO. Thank you, Ambassador.

Brian?

Mr. WHITMORE. If I may just jump in one more time—in terms of where all this money is coming from, I think there is one place we really need to be looking, and this refers back to my comments about organized crime in my initial comments. I don't know how many people remember the case of Eston Kohver, the Estonian law enforcement officer who was kidnapped back in September 2015 and taken across the border to Russia. This was a very big case, very appalling, a European Union citizen being kidnapped from the territory of a European Union state, brought back to Russia and put on a show trial.

What was really, really telling about the Kohver case to me, however, was what Mr. Kohver was investigating. And I think this is crucial to understanding where this money comes from. Kohver was investigating a cigarette smuggling ring run out of eastern Estonia by Russian organized crime groups facilitated by the Federal Security Service of the Russian Federation.

Now at first glance, this just looks like some bent FSB guys getting rich off a cigarette smuggling ring. That's not what it was. In my conversations with Estonian law enforcement officials, what it was, was essentially creating a *chernaya kassa*, a black account.

Now if this is just one little cigarette smuggling ring, you multiply that across all of the operations going on that Russian organized crime is involved in, that are facilitated by the security services, you get a lot of untraceable cash. And you wonder where this money is going that is supporting xenophobic and far-right outfits across Europe, or supporting these so-called alternative media sites across Europe. And you begin to get a pretty good idea, because this gives the Kremlin a lot of money to play with, with no fingerprints on it. And I think this is one of the places we need to be looking.

Mr. MASSARO. Thanks, Brian.

Additional questions? Right there.

QUESTIONER. Hi. My name's Dale Amberger [sp]. I'm an intern for Congressman Josh Gottheimer.

Marius was talking about how instrumental this whole system is, the system of the KGB. Obviously, the cohort that's now in power went through the KGB. What's your assessment on the new guard? Because obviously they were not KGB trained. And is there any opportunity for us in the West to interact with these new emerging leaders?

Mr. MASSARO. I'm sorry. Who's your question for? Marius?

All right. Please.

Mr. LAURINAVIČIUS. Well, some of them are FSB trained, some of them not. But it's not just about the individuals. It's about the system. It's—KGB, from the very beginning it was—essentially, we make a mistake when we judge about the KGB as about some intelligence organization we have in the West. From the very beginning it was a criminal organization, not only because it controlled all the criminal world in the Soviet Union but because it has all kind of relations with terrorists, organized crime groups in the West and everywhere. And when I look at the nowadays situation, I really don't—looking back into KGB history, I don't see major differences and major new things. Only new things are some new tools, like social media or something like that. We're talking, let's say, about fake news. And we consider fake news a new phenomenon. Let's look back to the ideas like HIV was invented by CIA, or nuclear winter theory and many, many others—Pope XII collaboration with Nazis and many, many others. These are fake news which were invented decades ago, and now they're just doing the same thing using the new tools. That's it.

Mr. MASSARO. Yes. Dr. Aslund, willing to make a short comment?

Dr. ASLUND. Yes. well, this is not happening. What is happening is that there is a nationalization of a new elite. You can see three groups: technocrats, KGB officers, and nationalists.

Putin has said, very clearly, either you stay in Russia and get a Russian education, or you go abroad and you stay there.

Mr. MASSARO. Thank you.

So let's try to do one or two more questions. Right back there——

QUESTIONER. Hi. I'm an intern with Congressman Heck's office.

Mr. Whitmore, earlier you talked about how there are two aspects of the Russian regime. There's the corruption and the ideological aspect. Could you and anyone else maybe expand on sort of how those two aspects, the ideological and the corruption, work in concert?

Mr. WHITMORE. Yes. I can. When I talk about the ideological, I want to be clear I'm talking about Putin's project of making Russia a great power again, making Russia great again, if you will. And so in this sense, there's good and bad corruption. If you have corruption that's operating abroad and creating networks of influence that you can then use to undermine democratic institutions in the West, be they in the near abroad or farther west—and on this regard, I would say I would echo what Marius said earlier: Everything that we're experiencing now, they were experiencing before. And I think we should really, really pay very close attention to what Russia does to its neighbors, because it's often a harbinger of what they're going to be doing to us a little bit later. I mean, remember, the Estonians were getting hacked before it was cool. [Chuckles.] OK?

So this is corruption that works hand in glove with the ideological aims of the regime. When I described that complex ownership structure of this company called Vemex that is buying up energy assets in the Czech Republic, yeah, a lot of people are getting rich from this, and it's also advancing the interests of the state.

Where it's not—where they're working in competition with each other, where ideological Russia and kleptocratic Russia, if you will, are working at cross purposes, I think we began to see evidence of this about a year ago, when we began to see Putin start to cull his inner circle, when we saw people like Vladimir Yakunin, the former head of Russian Railways, once considered one of the most powerful men in Russia, lose his job; when we saw Viktor Ivanov, who was head of the so-called antinarcotics service—which was nothing of the sort—but anyway, we saw him lose his job; when we saw Sergei Ivanov, the former Kremlin chief of staff, lose his job, this I interpreted as Putin basically trying to rein in some of the more kleptocratic elements of his inner circle, bringing in younger people who are going to be willing to steal less and work a little bit harder, essentially, if you will.

So I think this was an attempt by ideological Russia to rein in kleptocratic Russia, because, let's face it, rebuilding an empire is very expensive. And this tension, I think, is something we always kind of need to keep our eye on, between these two Russias that, again, like I said, sometimes are working hand in glove but sometimes are working at cross purposes.

Mr. MASSARO. And on that, we'll conclude the briefing. Thank you so much, Brian. Thank you so much to the full panel. A fascinating briefing. And we'll see you all at the next one. [Applause.]

[Whereupon, at 4:59 p.m., the briefing ended.]

Æ

This is an official publication of the **Commission on Security and Cooperation in Europe.**

★ ★ ★

This publication is intended to document developments and trends in participating States of the Organization for Security and Cooperation in Europe (OSCE).

★ ★ ★

All Commission publications may be freely reproduced, in any form, with appropriate credit. The Commission encourages the widest possible dissemination of its publications.

★ ★ ★

www.csce.gov   @HelsinkiComm

The Commission's Web site provides access to the latest press releases and reports, as well as hearings and briefings. Using the Commission's electronic subscription service, readers are able to receive press releases, articles, and other materials by topic or countries of particular interest.

Please subscribe today.

Printed in Great Britain
by Amazon